D0431692

MILLIPEDEOLOGY

by Michael Elsohn Ross

photographs by Brian Grogan • illustrations by Darren Erickson

Carolrhoda Books, Inc. / Minneapolis

To the Magners and their millipedes

Many thanks to Carl Brownless and the students at El Portal Elementary School, El Portal, California, and the students of Third Ward School, Griffin, Georgia

Additional photographs courtesy of: © Robert and Linda Mitchell, pp. 7, 26, 31, 46.

Text copyright © 2000 by Michael Elsohn Ross
Photographs copyright © 2000 by Carolrhoda Books, Inc.
Illustrations copyright © 2000 by Carolrhoda Books, Inc.

This book is available in two editions:
Library binding by Carolrhoda Books, Inc.
Soft cover by First Avenue Editions
Divisions of Lerner Publishing Group
241 First Avenue North, Minneapolis, MN 55401 U.S.A.

Website address: www.lernerbooks.com

LIBRARY OF CONGRESS CATALOGING-IN-PUBLICATION DATA

Ross, Michael Elsohn, 1952–
    Millipedeology / by Michael Elsohn Ross ; photographs by Brian Grogan ; illustrations by Darren Erickson.
        p.   cm.—(Backyard buddies)
    Summary: Describes the physical characteristics and behavior of the millipede and presents millipede-related activities.
    ISBN 1-57505-398-5 (hardcover: alk. paper)
    ISBN 1-57505-436-1 (pbk.: alk. paper)
    1. Millipedes—Juvenile literature. [1. Millipedes.] I. Grogan, Brian, 1951– ill. II. Erickson, Darren, ill. III. Title. IV. Series: Ross, Michael Elsohn, 1952– Backyard buddies.
QL449.6.R27 2000
595.6'6—dc21   99-35398

Manufactured in the United States of America
1 2 3 4 5 6 – JR – 05 04 03 02 01 00

Contents

If I could dance like a millipede,

I'd cruise at low speed.

Leaving footprints in the street,

I'd tickle the world beneath my feet.

Greet the millipede. Perhaps you've watched a millipede cruise along backyard trails, but have you ever stopped to introduce yourself?

Millipedes do not sting or bite. Sometimes they do make a stink, however, to protect themselves from enemies. The stinky substance of certain tropical millipedes can irritate the skin, but you won't run into this—unless you live in a tropical rain forest.

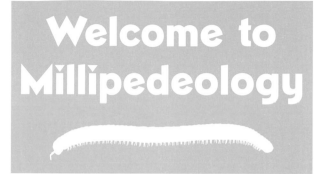

Welcome to Millipedeology

Some folks are frightened by the common millipedes they meet at home, but there's no reason to fear these little critters.

Ichthyologists study fish and psychologists study minds. Millipedeologists unravel the mysteries of their many-legged neighbors. You don't need a license to be a millipedeologist. Just follow your curiosity down the winding path to the land of millipedes.

If you are anxious to find some millipedes, just get a small plastic container and go outdoors. Since millipedes are out at night, you can usually find them resting during the day. Look under rocks, boards, the bark of dead trees, or piles of moist, dead leaves. Don't be a home wrecker! Be sure to replace rocks and anything else you search under. Most millipedes prefer to live in damp places, but some kinds actually live in the desert. Millipedes live in cities, too. If you don't have a backyard, try looking for them in a community garden, vacant lot, or park.

As you search for millipedes, you may encounter centipedes as well. These close relatives of millipedes have stingers on their tail end.

Millipede Hunt

Though their sting can be painful, you are too big to be seriously harmed by them. On the other hand, you are big enough to hurt small critters like centipedes and millipedes if you are not careful with them. Be a gentle giant.

When you find a millipede, you can steer it into your container with a leaf or stick. Sunlight can harm the leggy creature, so keep your container hidden away in the shade.

Think about how your family members might feel about having a millipede as a houseguest. Before marching indoors with your new buddy, you might want to show your folks the following article from the *Garden Gazette* (an important make-believe newspaper).

THE GARDEN GAZETTE

QUIET GUESTS

When Hannah and Danny Dolittle of Wizard Wells, Texas, asked if they could study a wild critter at home, their ma replied, "I don't want any armadillos rolled up in the hall or any snakes slithering through the kitchen. Forget about bats, buzzards, and bunnies, too." Hannah and Danny were at a loss as to what they could watch, until one day they discovered a long and lovely millipede traveling across the backyard. They followed it in fascination and finally invited it home. Ma Dolittle approved of their new pal. "Why, I can't see anything wrong with it," she said. "It's quiet and small, and it can live in a jar." Which is what it did, until the kids set it free a few days later.

Life under a pile of leaves or in a rotten log can be quite cozy, at least if you're a millipede! To keep your millipede guests in comfort, collect some of the materials listed below and follow the instructions for making a millipede motel. See page 27 for some ideas on what you should include for your millipedes to eat.

sprinkle the water into the container to keep the soil moist. Millipedes need a moist home, not a dry or soggy one.

4. The motel is now ready for lodgers. Invite some millipedes in for a visit.

5. Make a sign that says, "Millipede Motel," to let the people you live with know they have guests.

Warning: Keep the motel in a cool place. Heat from a lamp or direct sunlight can be harmful to millipedes.

6. Remember that motels are only temporary homes. After you have enjoyed your guests for a week, return them to their real home.

You will need:

✔ millipedes
✔ a coffee can or plastic container with a lid that has holes punched in it
✔ a handful of moist, dead leaves
✔ moist soil
✔ a bottle cap

What to Do:

1. Fill the container with 2 to 3 inches of soil. This will give your millipedes room to burrow.
2. Lay a blanket of moist leaves on top of the soil. This will give your millipedes some shelter.
3. Once a day, fill the bottle cap with water and

Inside Secrets

Sneak a peek at your millipede guests. What are they up to in their new home? Perhaps, like a spy, you can discover some secrets of millipede life. Grab a notepad and pen. Each time you notice your guests up to something new, record your observations. Challenge your family and friends to see what they can discover by peering into the motel.

Like a true spy, check out the activities of your subjects at different times. Maybe they are more active in the morning or the evening. Keep track of the time as you jot down each new discovery. To keep aware of millipede movements, sketch their exact location in the jar each time you take a peek.

What kind of playground would you need if you had many feet? What do you think a millipede might like? In a large baking pan or dish tub, create a wild and wacky playground for your guests. (Be sure to get permission before using things that belong to someone else!)

Milli-Playground

Arrange the items listed (except the notepad and pencil) in the pan or tub. Set a millipede in the playground and watch it carefully. What does it do when it finds new pieces of playground equipment? Does it seem to like one place better than another? Jot down some notes to help you remember the millipede's actions.

Gently touch the millipede. How does it react? If you have any more millipedes, place them in the playground. Do they notice each other? What do they do when they meet? Watch the millipedes. Do they all react to things in the same way? Do some of them react differently?

Be sure to return your guests to their motel after they have crawled about for a while. Your folks might not be too pleased if they discover your millipedes using the rest of the house as a playground!

You will need:

- ✔ millipedes
- ✔ a large baking pan or dish tub
- ✔ stems
- ✔ leaves
- ✔ small toys (cars, marbles)
- ✔ a small mirror
- ✔ pieces of yarn or string
- ✔ an empty spool of thread and a Popsicle stick (to make a seesaw)
- ✔ a small pile of dirt
- ✔ anything else you can think of
- ✔ notepad and pencil

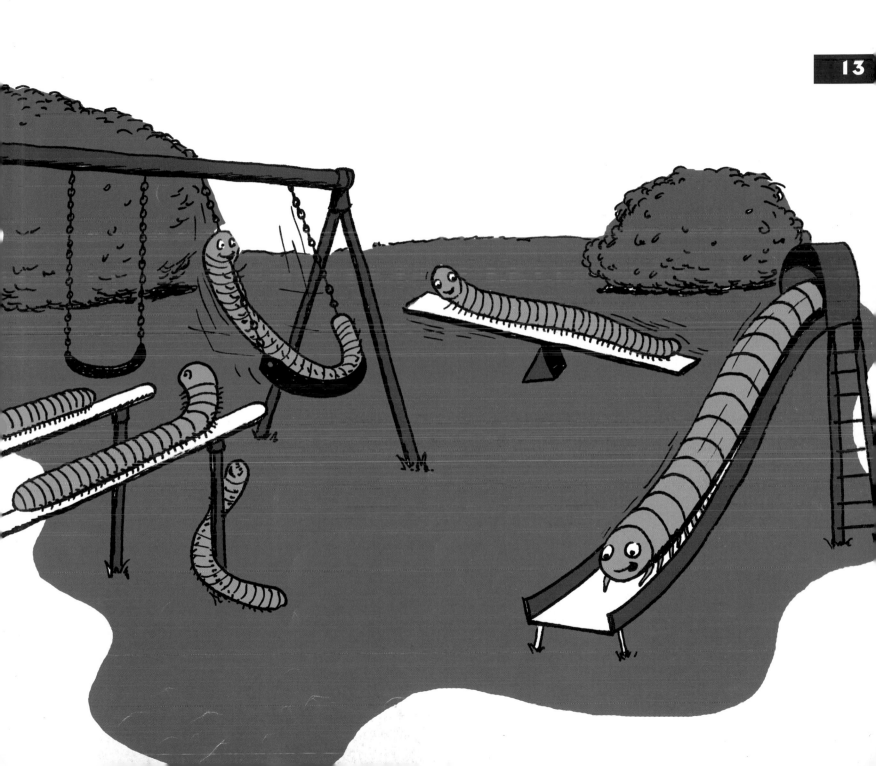

Aware Dare

Are you aware? Would you notice if your neighbor got a new car or your dog wore a dress? Would you notice if your teacher got braces? Do you pick up on small details? Whatever your answers, the Aware Dare is for you. If you are completely tuned out, this game will help you tune in to tiny details. Being tuned in is extremely helpful when you are becoming familiar with new friends, such as millipedes. On the other hand, if you are totally aware, this game will allow you to show off your sharp wits. Although it can be played alone, the Aware Dare is more challenging with two or more players.

You will need:

✔ a millipede
✔ a clear drinking glass or plastic container
✔ a leaf
✔ a magnifying lens
✔ optional: a pen or pencil and paper

How to Play:

1. Place a millipede in the glass along with the leaf.

2. Decide who is going to go first.

3. Beginning with player number one, take turns using the magnifying lens to look closely at the millipede and then sharing an observation. For example, someone might say, "It has a lot of legs," or "It wiggles." Any detail is okay, but no repeats are allowed. More details can be added to someone else's observations, however. For example, if someone says, "It has a lot of legs," someone else can say, "It has short legs."

Optional: Pick one player to record what each of you notices.

4. Continue taking turns in the same order until only one player is able to make a new observation. The last person to share a millipede detail is the most aware.

5. Return the millipede to its motel or to the outdoors.

Millipedes are very mathematical. Though we don't know if they can multiply or divide, we do know that we discover more about them through mathematical explorations. The millipede's name means "one thousand feet" (*mille* means "one thousand" and *ped* means "feet"). Do they really have a thousand feet? Find out for yourself.

Mathipede

segments that do not have legs. You'll find these at the tail end. Subtract these segments from the total number of segments. To find the total number of legs on your millipede, multiply the number of segments with legs by the number of legs on each segment.

Shape Changers: As you watch your millipede, you may notice that its body forms a variety of shapes as it moves about. Sketch some of the different shapes you notice. Millipedes often curl up. How many spiral turns do you see in your millipede's curl?

Paired Parts: Besides having legs in pairs, are there any other parts that millipedes wear in pairs? Do they have two ears or two tails? Use a magnifying lens to search your millipede carefully for paired parts.

Time Test: How fast or slow is your millipede pal? Place it in the center of a piece of paper, then use the watch or clock to time it. See how long it takes to crawl off. Time your millipede to see how long it will stay curled after it has been pestered. What other time tests can you think of?

Color Count: Some people might look at a millipede and notice just one color. But bug detectives like you can notice the fine details of color by looking at a millipede closely with a magnifying lens. Can you match the colors you see on your millipede with colors in your crayon box?

You will need:

✔ a millipede
✔ several sheets of paper and a pencil
✔ a magnifying lens
✔ a watch or clock
✔ crayons

Foot Count: Counting each little foot on your millipede could be quite a chore. Luckily there is an easier way to count feet. Check out the number of legs on each **segment,** or ring. Do you see that there are two legs on each side? Using a pencil as a pointer, count the number of segments on your millipede. Then count the number of

Artists sometimes have to search for a long time before they find the right model for a portrait. Perhaps more artists would be satisfied if they chose millipedes for models. As you probably have noticed, millipedes pose in interesting postures. Sometimes they drape themselves over a stick or curl up on a leaf. You might want to use a millipede for a model the next time you draw a picture.

The Model Model

You will need:

✔ a millipede
✔ a pencil and several sheets of scrap paper
✔ a magnifying lens
✔ small toys or other props
✔ crayons, paints, or colored pencils

What to Do:

Using your toys, pose your millipede as a space alien, a giant bug on a highway, or anything else you want.

Fly with Your Eyes: Using the magnifying lens, pretend you are a spy plane zooming over the millipede. Carefully examine its colors, shapes, parts, and other details, such as bumps and ridges.

Snapshot: Make some quick, simple sketches of the different things that you notice, such as the shape of its tail end or the placement of its head.

Regard Your Curiosity: If questions such as "What is that thing called?" pop into your brain, jot them down next to your drawings. Questions are well worth collecting—they might come in handy later in this book.

Almost There . . . : Before making your final picture, do some sketches of the basic shape of the millipede. This will help you experiment with the drawing before working on the fine details.

Bigger than Life: A life-size drawing of a millipede is a challenge both to draw and to look at. It's easier to include small details when you make your artwork big. Give your portrait plenty of room.

Art Show: Be proud of your creation. Display your portrait at a local art museum, at your neighborhood library, or on the family fridge.

Do you wonder about millipedes? Some kids in El Portal, California, and Griffin, Georgia, did. Here are some of their questions:

Are millipedes dangerous? How do they protect themselves? Why do they make a stink? How long do they live? How many legs do they have? How many rings do they have?

Can they dig holes or swim? Can they go faster than an inchworm? A cheetah? How fast can millipedes climb? Can they change forms like a caterpillar? Can millipedes survive in water? Can they burrow?

Do they have backbones? Antennae? Teeth? Stingers? Noses?

What do they eat? How much do they eat? Would they get itchy if they ate poison oak? What do they weigh? How long do they get? How many kinds are there? Are they related to caterpillars? Centipedes?

Where do millipedes live? Why is their skin white when they shed it? Do they migrate? How are they affected by different seasons? How do they find their way around? How do they react to cold? Can they survive during winter? Why do millipedes come into the bathroom at school?

Are you ready to chart unexplored territory? Are you prepared to dive into the unknown? If you are, all you need to do is to follow a millipede question. Is there something you really wonder about millipedes? Yes? Well, let that question lead you on a journey. Below are some tips for millipedeologists with questions.

Follow That Question

—**Research:** Other millipedeologists may have asked your question already. Perhaps the answer to your question lies in a book. It may even be in this one. Turn the page and search through the next section. If that doesn't work, look at some other books. If you need to experiment to answer your question—read on.

—**Scrutinize:** Could you answer your question through closer observation? For example, if your question was, "Do millipedes have antennae?" do you think you might be able to find any by looking at a millipede through a magnifying lens?

—**Find an Expert:** Do you know a bug expert? Perhaps a local gardener, agricultural advisor, or college instructor can give you a hand. Advice may be only a phone call away.

—**Experiment:** Questions often lead to experiments. What would happen if . . . ? Could you answer your question with an experiment? The chapter called Kid Experiments, starting on page 35, has stories about experiments conducted by other bold millipedeologists. These kids may inspire you to roll up your sleeves and set up your very own experiment.

Look at this millipede. Can you find eyes, teeth, or ears? Can you find legs, wings, or a stinger? Does it have parts that are different from yours?

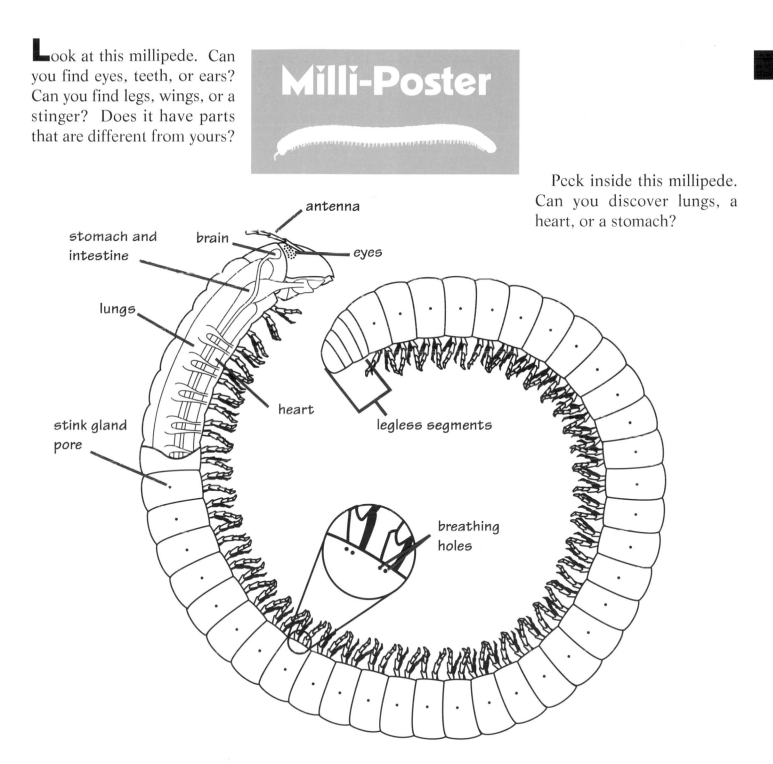

Milli-Poster

Pcck inside this millipede. Can you discover lungs, a heart, or a stomach?

antenna

stomach and intestine

brain

eyes

lungs

heart

stink gland pore

legless segments

breathing holes

What Is It?

What has rings like a worm but more legs than an octopus? What has claws like an eagle but protects itself like a skunk? What makes a nest like a bird but burrows like a mole? Would you guess a millipede?

Millipedes are similar to all these animals, but their closest relatives are centipedes. If you have checked out millipedes up close, you may have noticed that most of their segments have two pairs of legs. Animals with two sets of legs on each segment are called **diplopods** (DIP-loh-pahdz). *Diplo* means "two" and *pod* means "foot." Centipedes also have many segments, but they have only one pair of legs per body part. Both millipedes and centipedes belong to a bigger group of animals called **myriapods** (MEER-ee-ah-pahdz).

Myriapods are part of an even larger group of animals called **arthropods.** *Arthro* means "joint" and *pod* means "foot." All arthropods have jointed legs. Ants, butterflies, lobsters, spiders, and scorpions are all arthropods and distant cousins of the millipede.

Check out your millipede and your millipede portraits. Does your millipede fit the description of a diplopod, a myriapod, and an arthropod?

Arthropods are creatures with pairs of jointed legs. The animals below are arthropods.

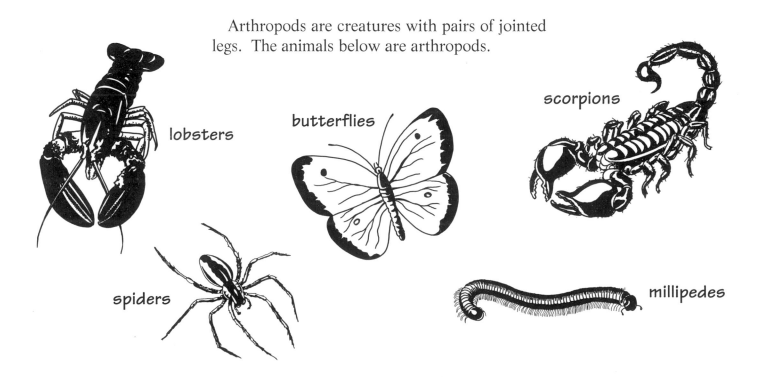

lobsters

butterflies

scorpions

spiders

millipedes

Myriapods are arthropods with many segments of the same shape and many legs.

centipedes

millipedes

Diplopods are myriapods with two pairs of legs on each segment.

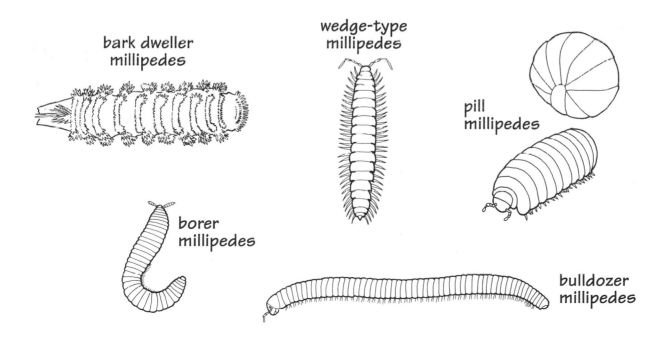

bark dweller millipedes

wedge-type millipedes

pill millipedes

borer millipedes

bulldozer millipedes

Aha, Tusenfoting... Say What?

Each language has its own name for millipedes. In Hawaiian the word for millipedes is *aha*. In Swedish, it's *tusenfoting*. In Pilipino, it's *alupihan*. Is the little creature an *aha*, a *tusenfoting*, an *alupihan*, or a millipede? To avoid using all these names, scientists have come up with a worldwide system of naming all living things. Whether you live in Hawaii, Sweden, or the Philippines, there is only one scientific name for each **species**, or kind, of millipede.

Latin and Greek, the ancient languages of Rome and Greece, are used in creating scientific names. Did you know that we call most dinosaurs by their scientific names? When you say *Seismosaurus*, you are saying "earthshaking lizard." If you can say dinosaur names, you can certainly say the scientific names of millipedes. Impress your friends by saying the name of the American millipede called *Narceus americanus* (NAR-say-us ah-may-rih-CAN-us). It is the largest millipede found in North America.

Cleanup Crew

Every day, plants drop old leaves, flowers, twigs, and branches. These discards would make piles many feet deep if it weren't for nature's cleanup crew. If you look among plant litter, you'll discover worms, beetles, maggots, and millipedes busy munching this material into smaller bits. This broken-down plant matter is one of the main parts of topsoil, the rich layer of soil on the surface. Without the topsoil from recycled plant parts, young plants would not grow well.

In most places, earthworms are the most important **decomposers,** or recyclers, of plant material. But when earthworms are scarce, millipedes fill in. In such situations, there may be several hundred millipedes per square yard of soil. These hungry millipedes may consume as much as one-quarter of all the plant litter that falls in their habitat.

Most millipedes eat leaves and wood. Some kinds of millipedes may be picky about what types of food they eat. Millipedes that prefer the tender roots of young seedlings can be pests to sugar beet farmers. **Fungi,** plantlike organisms that eat decaying matter, are a favorite food of some millipedes. Scientists found one millipede with 76 species of fungi in its digestive system!

In experiments, scientists discovered that pill millipedes preferred leaves coated with fungi and other organisms to leaves that had been washed clean. These organisms not only help make the food easier to digest, but also provide extra nutrition.

In order for some types of millipedes to get all the nutrients they need, they must pass food through their digestive system twice. Yes, this means that they have to eat their own droppings (poop). Other millipedes eat the algae that grows on bark or on dead animals, such as snails.

Have your parents ever said, "If you want to be big and strong, eat your vegetables"? For millipedes, not eating enough good food may lead to a longer youth. The poorer the food, the slower they develop—and the longer it takes them to grow up!

Milli-Sense

Have you ever noticed that a millipede taps its **antennae** the way a person who is blind may tap a cane? Antennae are sense organs found on the heads of many millipedes and other animals. Millipede antennae come well-equipped with sensors that can taste foods, sniff out odors, and feel whatever is in front of them. Scientists think that millipede antennae also have sensors that can measure temperature and find water. Using this fancy equipment, millipedes can avoid hot sunlight, discover moist places to hang out, and find food.

A millipede has two or more eyes on each side of its head. These eyes detect light and movement, helping millipedes find their way around. Millipedes may also use the moon or other lights in the sky for navigation.

Since millipedes, like other arthropods, have a hard skin, they sense the outside world through hairs that grow out of their protective shield. Tickle the hairs on your millipede. What happens?

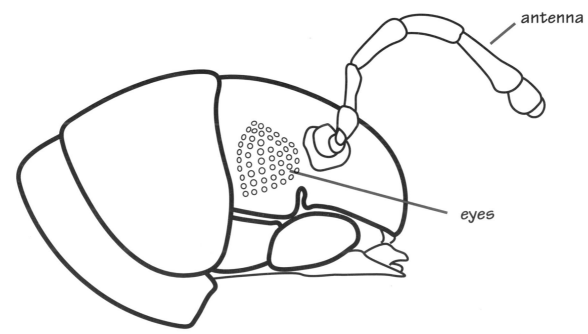

antenna

eyes

Dozer Heads

Have you ever tripped over your own feet? Imagine you had hundreds of feet like a millipede. Would you be clumsy? If you watch a millipede cruise along the ground, you'll seldom see one trip. As a millipede walks, each pair of legs moves together, but the pair in front and back on each segment step at a slightly different time. This rhythmic motion looks like a series of waves and prevents the legs from getting in each other's way.

Millipedes don't wear rock-climbing shoes, but they do have special claws on their feet that help them climb trees and even walk upside down! Each step begins with a millipede grasping the surface with its claws and then pushing backward with its legs. This moves the body forward. With two sets of legs per segment, a millipede is like a truck with two sets of tires.

Using the power of its many legs and hard, bulldozer-like head, a millipede is able to plow through soil and under bark. This movement would compress a millipede's body like an accordion if it weren't made of hard rings. A millipede can move from side to side and up and down, but when its head is pressed into the soil, its body becomes as stiff as a metal rod.

Could you picture yourself saddled up on a galloping millipede? Mites, the most numerous of tiny soil animals, often hitch rides on millipedes to travel at high speed to new lands. Some millipedes may have 50 or more of these hitchhikers clinging to their legs or rings at one time.

Saved by the Smell

Some folks think millipedes stink. Sniff yours. What does it smell like? Some smell like camphor, a substance that comes from plants and is used to keep certain insects away. In fact, some kinds of millipedes make their very own bug repellent, which is similar to camphor. When this millipede "juice" was applied to cockroaches, it caused them to start scratching.

The pill millipede, found in Europe and the southern United States, oozes a special chemical from glands on its back. This chemical makes the animals that attack the millipede sleepy. The wolf spider, a hunter of small critters, is particularly sensitive to the chemical. Most wolf spiders that attack and begin to eat pill millipedes get put to sleep for at least 12 hours. This doesn't always save the millipede that was attacked, but it does help its millipede neighbors.

Other millipedes produce cyanide (SYE-uh-nide), a poison that is deadly to tiny bugs that eat or even breathe it. This chemical defense works to keep away most predators, including groups of fire ants. Although most of these chemicals work best to protect millipedes from other small creatures, some tropical millipedes can shoot defensive sprays a foot away. Millipedeologists think this means that these millipedes might also repel larger animals, such as birds, mammals, and lizards. Though the poisons are usually not strong enough to do any serious harm to larger creatures, one millipede species has been known to kill lizards. And people use some species of tropical millipedes to make poison for arrowheads.

Not all millipedes use chemicals to defend themselves. Some roll up and protect themselves like hedgehogs or armadillos. The African pill millipede rolls into a tight sphere the size of a golf ball and is protected from most enemies by its hard shell. But mongooses (furry animals that have pointed noses and are about the size of a house cat) have learned to kill African pill millipedes by smashing them against rocks! Millipedes are also eaten by hedgehogs, shrews, frogs, turtles, beetles, scorpions, and some species of ants.

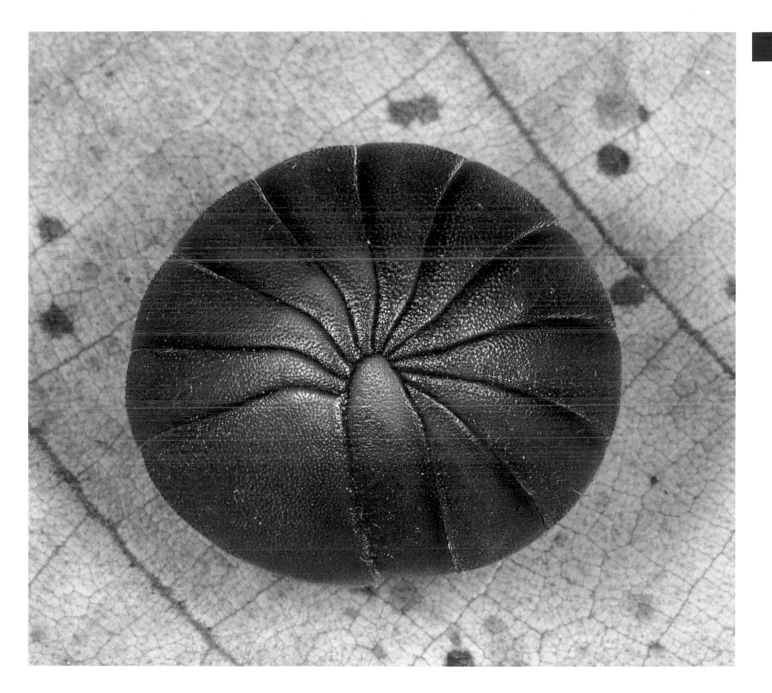

Making Millipedes

Though millipedes may often be munched by other creatures, more millipedes are being made all the time. Male and female millipedes must first find each other so they can create baby millipedes. Certain species rely on music to attract a mate. The males may drum on the ground or rub their legs against their body like a cricket does. One species of female is offered a sweet treat that oozes from glands on the male. After lapping up this dessert, she is ready to mate. Another species attracts the female by making a silk thread, which she then follows to the mating site. At least one species of female millipede appears to attract the male by releasing an irresistible perfume.

The mating act of most millipedes begins with the male climbing up on the female's back and then holding tight. Mating may last a few minutes or several hours. During this time, the male passes the female a packet of **sperm.** She stores this in a special compartment on her underside until she is ready to **fertilize** her eggs, which makes them able to grow. Some female millipedes may mate only once and use the sperm from these stored packets to fertilize as many as one thousand eggs. Females of several European species of millipedes can produce female young without mating at all. Very few males, if any, of these species are found in the wild.

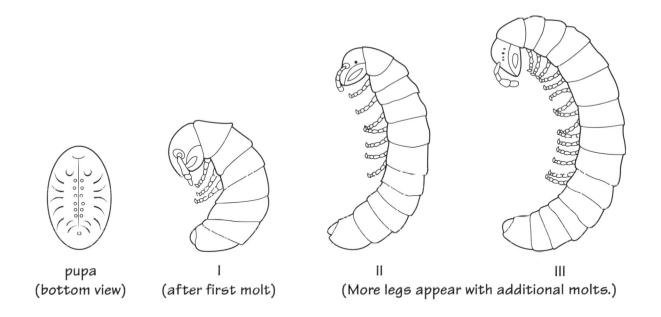

| pupa
(bottom view) | I
(after first molt) | II | III
(More legs appear with additional molts.) |

Females lay from 10 to 300 eggs at one time in holes in the ground. Many millipedes make a nestlike container for their eggs out of soil, chewed-up leaves, silk, or droppings. These "nests" protect the eggs from extreme changes in temperature and moisture. The eggs usually hatch after several weeks. In one species, the female actually gives the male the eggs to keep in a special pouch in his body until they are ready to hatch. But most millipedes let their eggs hatch on their own.

Before hatching, the young millipede goes through several changes inside the egg. When the egg is laid, the young, legless millipede looks like a small worm. Within a day, the millipede **molts,** or sheds its skin, and it looks like a small cater-pillar with three pairs of legs. Since a millipede's skin is hard like a shell, it must continue to molt in order to grow. Between molts, the millipede may also develop body parts, such as legs. Within another day, the young millipede molts again. By this time, it has more legs and segments, as well as stink glands and eyes. The millipede may have only one pair of legs on some segments and two pairs of legs on others. Most millipedes chew their way out of their egg case at this stage in their development.

As millipedes grow, they continue to molt. With each molt, they have more legs and segments. Many species take 2 to 4 years to reach maturity. Some have been known to survive for 11 years!

Amazing Millipedes

Researchers believe that the first millipedes appeared on Earth about four hundred million years ago. Along with scorpions, they were one of the very first animals to live on dry land. During the days of the dinosaurs, millipedes the size of surfboards roamed forests of giant mosses. They were the largest animals without backbones ever to have walked on Earth.

Many people may think the millipedes they find are odd creatures, with their many legs and gliding movements. But even more unusual millipedes exist. In Sierra Leone, Africa, there are millipedes that jump an inch or more when disturbed. If you live in California, you may have seen millipedes that glow like fireflies. They can be seen from 30 feet away and are sometimes found in such large numbers that they look like a starry sky on a dark night. When they are handled, the millipedes glow even brighter.

Though army ants on a march attack most animals they run across, many millipedes have been seen marching unharmed among these ants. It is thought that the millipedes serve as sanitation workers, cleaning up mold and other messes. Millipedes that can survive for months underwater, grazing on tiny plants, live along the Amazon River. Millipedes found in caves are blind and have long legs and antennae. Some tropical species of millipedes live in greenhouses in northern parts of the world, where they've ended up after hitching a ride in the soil of imported tropical plants.

In the southern United States, millipedes may swarm into basements or under front doors after heavy rains. In Japan, one type of millipede has earned the name "train millipede" because of its tendency to swarm in large numbers onto railroad tracks. Sometimes there are such large numbers of these critters that the trains can't move ahead until the millipedes have been removed. In 1949, an estimated 65 million millipedes swarmed across 75 acres of farmland in West Virginia, like a huge crowd of people at a rock concert. Cattle gave up trying to find grass to eat, and wells filled with dead millipedes. During the night and on cloudy days, they moved ahead. No one was sure where they were going or where they came from, but they were killed by hot sunlight after a few days.

Though millipedes may sometimes be pests, they may also be of great help to people. A group of researchers has discovered that extracts of chemicals from one species of millipede can stop the growth of cancer cells for up to 6 hours. Perhaps millipedes can provide cures for some of the diseases that plague us.

Kid Experiments

How Do Millipedes Respond to Light?

What do you do when a flashlight is shined in your face? Rico and Nick R. wondered what a millipede would do in response to a flashlight beam. They set a millipede inside a box with a hole in the lid and then went into the boys' bathroom without turning on the light. It was very dark. They conducted five tests. During each one, they placed the millipede in the center of the box and then shined the flashlight at it. Below are the results:

Test #1: crawled under flap in the box

Test #2: hid in corner

Test #3: hid in corner

Test #4: crawled around light and up flashlight to escape

Test #5: went to corner and lay flat

From this experiment, the boys decided that millipedes don't like light. What do you think?

What's a Millipede's Speed?

How fast could you go if you had hundreds of legs? Alex, Nick B., and Carroll made a millipede racetrack between four yardsticks on the sidewalk. Each time they released a millipede, Alex kept the time and Nick measured the distance covered in one minute. Here are the results that Carroll recorded:

Test #1: 1.69 yards

Test #2: 2.19 yards

Test #3: 1.78 yards

Test #4: 1.52 yards

At the fastest speed, the boys calculated that their millipede was traveling at .08 miles per hour. At that rate, it would take more than 12 hours to travel a mile. That's 60 times slower than it takes most kids to run a mile!

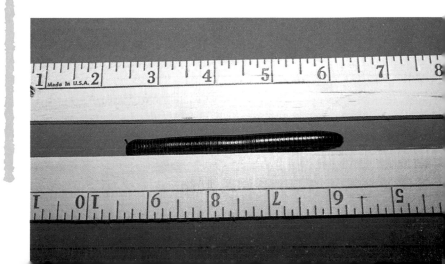

How Do Millipedes React to Different Temperatures?

What if a millipede on a winter stroll found itself on ice? What would it do? Nalani, Jamie, and Candice placed a millipede on ice cubes and noticed that it immediately trotted away. When they put it in a small bowl with several ice cubes, the millipede tried to get away, but then began to slow down and acted like it was taking a rest. Worried that it might be harmed, the girls removed it from the container. They thought that it might die if it had to stay on the ice any longer, so they chose to stop the experiment.

In another experiment, Alison and Nicole placed a millipede in a small plastic container inside a warm bowl. The air temperature in the bowl was 70° F. They repeated this test two more times, and these are their results:

Test #1: was restless and squirmy

Test #2: crawled fast

Test #3: crawled very fast

They also cooled off a bowl with ice and placed the millipede inside in its plastic container. The air temperature was 50° F. Here are the results:

Test #1: slow and motionless

Test #2: crawled slowly, trying to get out

Test #3: slow

The girls decided that millipedes are speeded up by heat and slowed down by cold.

Where Will Millipedes Go?

Leann and Brianna placed three piles of different kinds of soil on a round tray. On top of the soil, they arranged a variety of different kinds of leaves. In the center of the tray was a chunk of rotten wood. There wasn't any soil under the wood.

They released their millipede several times. Here's where it went:

Test #1: sand and yellow leaf

Test #2: red dirt

Test #3: black dirt

During each of the first three tests, the millipede continued to wander, and eventually it went off the tray. On the fourth test, however, something entirely different happened.

Test #4: went under log and stayed 20 seconds, then left the tray

Test #5: went under log for 25 seconds

Test #6: went under log for 22 seconds

Leann wondered if the millipede was looking for something under the log. She rearranged the tray so that the log had a portion of each kind of dirt underneath. This is what the millipede did on the next test:

Test #7: went under log and stayed there for 5 minutes

When the girls checked under the log, they discovered that the millipede was digging in the red dirt. They took the millipede out and put it back on the tray to see what it would do the next time. This time, it went under a sycamore leaf that was on the red dirt and stayed there. During other tests, the millipede again went under the log. When they tried the test with another millipede, it also went under the log.

Leann and Brianna concluded, "You won't find millipedes in sand, but you might find them on Saddle Hill (where the red dirt came from) under dead logs. They really like moist places." They also noted, "When millipedes move, they push dirt behind them."

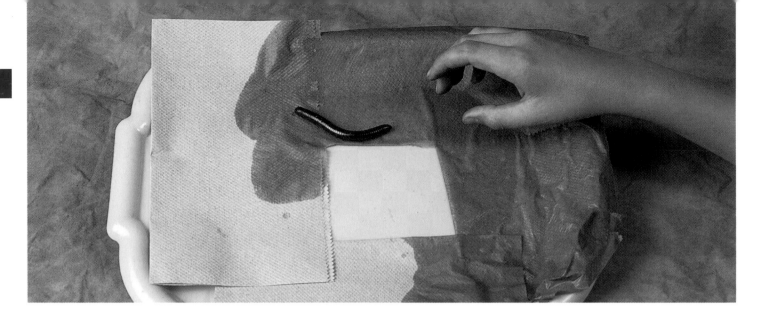

What Can a Millipede Climb?

Ali and Elizabeth took their millipede on a tour to discover what it could climb. It could not climb a big rock or a plastic pipe. It could climb a tree, a chair leg, Ali's hand, and a basketball. What else do you think a millipede could climb?

Do Millipedes React to Pressure from Air?

Kyle noticed that millipedes were often curled up. Did they curl up because of wind? To find out, he blew on his millipede several times. Here are his results:

Test #1: no reaction
Test #2: walked into the wind
Test #3: walked with the wind

Kyle isn't sure why millipedes curl up, but he doesn't think it has to do with air pressure.

Will a Millipede Go to Water?

Rhyen released his millipede between two folded paper towels. One was wet and the other was dry. The millipede turned toward the dry towel, but then faced the wet one and marched right to it. It walked around the wet towel, and when it got to the edge of the wet towel, it walked away. But it returned to the wet towel a little bit later. This was repeated six more times. Finally, it left the wet towel and went to the dry towel, where it crawled inside a fold and curled up. Why do you think it went to the wet towel and stayed there for a while, but then went to the dry towel? Rhyen thought that maybe it was looking for a home that was both wet and dark, but it couldn't find a place like that. Since the millipede could not crawl under the wet towel, the millipede chose the fold of the dry towel.

Like most creatures, millipedes need water to survive. When people get dry and thirsty, they look for something to drink. Robert O'Neill, a zoologist at the University of Illinois, wondered what millipedes do when they get dry. He set up a series of experiments to discover some answers.

Dry and Die

In one test, he placed 2 groups of 12 millipedes each in a special chamber with very dry air. He checked them every 15 minutes. During the first hour, almost all the millipedes became very active. After 4 hours, they became less and less active, and soon most were curled up in spirals. O'Neill concluded that the millipedes became active at first to look for wetter conditions. When they were unable to get to a moist spot, they curled up to save what body moisture they had left. O'Neill observed that when a millipede is curled up, it has less of its body exposed to the dry air.

O'Neill was also curious how long it would take millipedes who had lost moisture to fill up again with water, like camels at a desert oasis. He weighed some millipedes before placing them in a drying chamber. After the millipedes were in this dry place for 4 hours, he weighed them again. This showed how much weight they had lost. Some had lost more than 10 percent of their body weight. That would be like a 100-pound kid losing 10 pounds between lunch and dinner.

When O'Neill placed some of these dried millipedes in plastic containers with air as moist as fog, they continued to lose weight. He then placed them in containers with a moist sponge, and they gained back half of their lost weight in just 4 hours. When he gave them some soggy wood to eat along with the sponge, they gained back all their weight in 4 hours. It seems that millipedes need to get water back into their bodies by drinking or by eating soggy food. They can't get the water they need just from moist air.

When millipedes get dried out, they actively seek cool, wet places where there is moist food to eat, just as a kid does after exercising on a hot summer day.

Heavy Metal Dinners

When scientist Helen Read conducted tests to discover the effect of heavy metals on millipedes, she wasn't testing their reaction to heavy metal rock music. She was, however, investigating their reaction to pollution. Heavy metals, such as lead, cadmium, and zinc, are found in forests and fields near factories in Great Britain and other industrialized countries. Do deposits of these metals affect the growth of millipedes? Read had seen a report by one scientist that showed there are more dead leaves and fewer millipedes in forests polluted by heavy metals.

Read and her colleague, M. H. Martin, collected leaves from a British forest contaminated with zinc, lead, and cadmium. They gave one group of millipedes uncontaminated leaves and fed another group the leaves polluted with heavy metals.

After a series of tests, they discovered that the millipedes dining on contaminated leaves not only ate less, but none of them lived more than a month. On the other hand, half of the millipedes fed uncontaminated leaves were alive after a month, and many were still alive several months later.

Can millipedes get used to eating polluted food? What will happen to the forests if there are no millipedes to help make new soil? These are questions that millipedeologists like Helen Read may be trying to answer at this very moment.

Mysteries of a Backyard Buddy

Although this is the last part of the book, it isn't the last word on millipedes. Remember those questions about millipedes you collected? Are all of them answered? Maybe this book is not big enough to answer everyone's millipede ponderings. Or perhaps there are too many questions to be answered by any one book. Maybe no one has ever asked your question before. It could be up to you to find the answer!

Easily answered questions are like little gifts, while hard-to-explore questions are real prizes. Consider your tough questions once more and imagine the crazy investigations they could lead to.

Below are some lingering prize questions that kids from El Portal, California, and Griffin, Georgia, may still be looking into right now.

What do millipedes weigh?

Why do millipedes come into the bathrooms at school?

Can they go faster than an inchworm?

Would millipedes get itchy if they ate poison oak?

What leftover questions do you have?

Glossary

antennae: sense organs found in pairs on the heads of certain animals, such as millipedes

arthropods: a group of animals that have no backbones, have bodies made of sections, and have jointed feet

decomposers: plants and animals that help break down dead materials into smaller pieces

diplopods: arthropods with two pairs of legs on each body section

fertilize: to bring sperm and egg together to create new life

fungi: nonflowering plantlike organisms that live on decaying matter

molt: to shed the skin

myriapods: arthropods with many legs and with segments, or rings, of the same shape

segment: a section of an animal's body

species: a group of animals with common traits, especially the ability to produce young like themselves

sperm: the fluid a male makes to fertilize a female's egg

Index

About the Author

For over twenty years, Michael Elsohn Ross has taught visitors to Yosemite National Park about the park's wildlife and geology. Mr. Ross, his wife, Lisa (a nurse who served nine seasons as a ranger-naturalist), and their son, Nick, have led other families on wilderness expeditions since Nick learned to crawl. Mr. Ross studied conservation of natural resources at the University of California at Berkeley, with a minor in entomology (the study of insects). Mr. Ross's other books for children include the Naturalist's Apprentice series, also published by Carolrhoda Books.

Mr. Ross makes his home on a bluff above the wild and scenic Merced River, at the entrance to Yosemite Park. His backyard is a haven for rolypolies, crickets, snails, worms, spiders, ladybugs, millipedes, and a myriad of other intriguing critters.